The obscurity, of Alchemy, is defined as an art which sought in particular to transmute base metals into gold and/or the search for and to find a method and path to a better self. This obscurity is expanded upon to provide a better understanding of the Art.

The Smaragdine Table teaches about the plan of God when put into effect when the Universe was originally contemplated.

Learn about the Author's view on the subjects of love and living life and the soul. See how the story of Pinocchio matches the drama of life.

Discover more about Nature, Body, Spirit, Enlightenment, the Universe.

Each of the twelve subjects in the contents of this work is written upon to generate enthusiasm to pursue further to penetrate the veil of obscurities that is beyond the power of perception: God.

A Compilation of Obscurities is written in such a manner to be easily assimilated and especially for those who are being introduced to these philosophies for the first time.

The writings within "A Compilation of Obscurities" is offer to expand basic knowledge on subjects considered common and yet uncommon and to spark an interest to generate an appetite for the search for more.

A COMPILIATION OF OBSECURITIES

Trebor Onairtas

BALBOA.
PRESS

A DIVISION OF HAY HOUSE

Balboa Press books may be ordered through booksellers or by contacting:

Balboa Press
A Division of Hay House
1663 Liberty Drive
Bloomington, IN 47403
www.balboapress.com
1-(877) 407-4847

Because of the dynamic nature of the Internet, any web addresses or links contained in this book may have changed since publication and may no longer be valid. The views expressed in this work are solely those of the author and do not necessarily reflect the views of the publisher, and the publisher hereby disclaims any responsibility for them.

The author of this book does not dispense medical advice or prescribe the use of any technique as a form of treatment for physical, emotional, or medical problems without the advice of a physician, either directly or indirectly. The intent of the author is only to offer information of a general nature to help you in your quest for emotional and spiritual well-being. In the event you use any of the information in this book for yourself, which is your constitutional right, the author and the publisher assume no responsibility for your actions.

Any people depicted in stock imagery provided by Thinkstock are models, and such images are being used for illustrative purposes only.
Certain stock imagery © Thinkstock.

ISBN: 978-1-4525-6132-5 (sc)
ISBN: 978-1-4525-6130-1 (e)

Library of Congress Control Number: 2012919614

Printed in the United States of America

Balboa Press rev. date: 10/24/2012

CONTENTS

1

FORWARD

<u>Obscurity</u> – That unknown something that can be brought to light. The obscurity above all obscurities is the subject beyond all perception, which is <u>GOD</u>.

This work is a compilation of literary material accumulated from various sources. The compiled material supplies intellectual and spiritual light on obscurities regarding the inscrutable subject: <u>GOD</u>.

Written herein is what was gleaned from extensive reading and study of numerous works deemed plausible, possible, and conceivable and assists in reducing the obscurities of the unknowns which were and still are a source of intrigue.

This work is written in such a manner that the material herein will hopefully be easily assimilated and conveyed without any intention to convince, without doubt, or uncertainty. This tendency stems from the belief that <u>no one</u> knows anything about anything for sure and those who do choose to be silent.

Hopefully, this work will generate enthusiasm for the reader to pursue beyond what has been written here and use this enthusiasm to penetrate the veil of obscurities regarding the subject that is beyond the power of perception: <u>GOD</u>.

The choice to read this book illustrates the amount of curiosity that exists regarding the obscure and the search to uncover the covered.

Throughout the course of this work, passages from other writings are offered whenever appropriate. These materials are not mine and do not claim or profess them to be.

ALCHEMY

Just what is this alchemy? The definition of alchemy in the dictionary states:

> *"An art which sought in particular to transmute basic metals into gold and/or the search for and to find a method and path to a better self."*

The word alchemy when heard by most people almost immediately turns them away because the word has a connotation of changing less precious metals, such as lead, into the more precious metal, gold. Even if this could be accomplished it would be difficult to convince anyone that such a feat was possible without demonstrating the process while they were present. So, for the most part, alchemy becoming something of which everyone should be aware is immediately dismissed merely by virtue of the sound of the word.

Now, let's examine exactly what alchemy really is and has to offer. It is true that alchemy is a process of transformation. However, the transformation is exclusively for the "change" of the gross characteristics in man to the fine attributes always associated with goodness.

Hermes Trismegistus speaks to this in the Smaragdine Table exhibited in this work. You see, the whole idea of the substantiality, God, conjuring up a male and female, a man and woman, was that they would obey all the laws coincidental with their establishment. This man and woman established as totally perfect species were expected to obey these laws absolutely in order to remain in infinite perfection. To complement this state of perfection the gift of free will was bestowed upon them.

Before long, this gift of free will was violated and as a consequence, the state of perfection was affected. This violation of free will came about by satisfying a desire of the senses. This satisfaction of the senses is frequently related to, as the temptation of eating the apple from the forbidden tree. The violation of the free will to satisfy the desire of the senses, changing the state of perfection to imperfection, initiated the alchemical process to change imperfection to perfection at which point *the self* and the substantiality are as originally established as *one*.

Now that it has been made clear to the mind that alchemy is the means to transform the imperfect into the perfect one would have to wonder just what must be done or what action taken to achieve this level of perfection.

In order for anyone to indicate just what the procedure is to achieve this state of perfection would mean that someone would have already achieved this level of perfection for the prescription of the method to be prescribed to be considered valid. Furthermore, finding someone with this status is tantamount to searching for a needle in a hay stack and even if found it may be difficult to be totally convinced that someone really achieved that level of perfection.

So, you ask, what must I do to get back to square one? It really is easy and yet not so easy. To start, Moses was given two tablets upon which the ten commandments were engraved. Obeying these rules is a good start. The hard part comes when trying to decide (free will) not to do things that are satisfying to the senses and you are unsure as to whether the desire is gratifying toward the transformation process.

Discouraging? Absolutely! "T'aint easy McGee!" (taken from the radio show Fibber McGee and Molly). But let us not get too discouraged. The substantiality fully recognizes the predicament you are in and based on the love for each and every one of us, tolerance is given to these mistakes, but by virtue of your thinking, what action was taken, may be a mistake and is an indication that the action should be avoided in the future.

It should be remembered that whatever is written here is merely my interpretation of how to get where it is you seek to be.

Based on the fact that the substantiality is not constrained by the time element and that a million years can pass by virtue of the substantiality "blinking an eye," so to speak, you will most likely be granted a multitude of opportunities to redeem yourself over and over again. This does not mean that constant violation to the given laws will not hinder you and cause a fall to a lower rung on the ladder of success as explained elsewhere in this work.

In writing the contents of this book, I find myself not in total comfort, because I have not achieved the ultimate goal. Consequently, it is difficult for me to prescribe anything for anyone to reach this achievement as I cannot claim the credentials to do so.

Nevertheless, I feel compelled to write this work only because I feel a sense of joy in knowing that I have shared what I believe to be beneficial and uplifting toward achieving this admirable and gratifying goal.

Finally, I have found the study of alchemy not only to be fascinating but captivating in that it sets a reachable goal that if met will provide me with the necessary tools to promote and disseminate excellence to all.

GOD, THE SUBSTANTIALITY

To start, I was brought up as a Catholic, and attended Sunday school. A catechism, a book containing a summary of principles of the church, was distributed to all the students.

The first principle in the catechism states: "God always was and always will be."

This statement set the mind into thinking that "God" is "something." Exactly what this something is, is not made clear. Therefore, the reader is left to conclude, just what is this "something", this "God."

The principle statement, "God always was, and always will be" is tantamount to saying that "God" exists, and is a fact that cannot be doubted. Moreover then, God is unmistakably evident, and absolutely something substantial.

A fundamental fact is that something that exists must exist somewhere. Therefore the substantiality, God, must exist wherever somewhere.

The bible states on many occasions, God was made visible to whomever in the form of fire. The incident of Moses and the burning bush is one example of "God" revealed in the form of fire.

So, since "<u>God</u>" was revealed to Moses and others as <u>fire</u>, it is plausible to assume that this something substantial is <u>fire</u>.

The fact that today, <u>fire</u> is still a total mystery and the fact that "<u>God</u>" is also a total mystery, all the more, substantiates credence that <u>God</u> and <u>fire</u> are one and the same.

The proposition that <u>God</u> and <u>fire</u> are synonomous is a likely probability brings up the fact that <u>fire</u> cannot exist without the presence of oxygen. This established fact dictates that this fire, this substantiality, exists in an environment that contains oxygen which is one of the elements contained in <u>air</u>.

So, thus far we have derived by deduction that God is substantial, a consuming fire and enveloped in a sea of air.

Fire defined by the dictionary:

> *"The active principle of combustion manifested*
> *by the evolution of <u>light</u> and <u>heat</u>."*

This definition reveals that fire is something <u>substantial</u> from which <u>light</u> and <u>heat</u> emanate.

So, added to the deductions that God is <u>substantial</u>, a consuming fire, enveloped in a sea of air also emanates <u>light</u> and <u>heat</u>.

An event that occurred in a Catholic church during holy mass further confirms the above stated "God" possessed qualities. Upon the alter were two lighted candles. Curiosity led to questioning a nun seated close by as to the reason for the candles. Out came a very aggressive response: *"The fire and light are symbols representing God. God is the fire and the light."* Apparently, the aggressive response was a reaction to why the question had to be asked in the first place.

The four basic elements; fire, air, water and earth are what the universe is composed. Thus far, fire and air have been identified to be associated with God.

Following is an attempt to explain how the other two elements, water and earth become associated with God also.

Condensation. The laws of physics have established that the combined association of fire, air and heat eventually lead to the condition that generates water by the process of condensation.

The fire, air and heat associated with God are the established ingredients necessary to generate condensation or water.

Condensation, water, added to the elements already established existing in the realm of God, the substantial substance, leaves only one element lacking to make up the four elements. That last element is matter or earth.

In order to establish a relationship of matter with God, it is essential to be fully acquainted with the definition of matter.

Matter defined by the dictionary:

"the substance of which physical objects are composed. Physical or corporeal substances, in general, whether solid, liquid or gaseous, as distinguished from incorporeal substances such as spirit or mind, or from qualities, actions and whatever occupies space."

A compelling manner in which to establish the association of matter with God is to recall the incident of Moses and the burning bush. The fire spoke to Moses establishing that God is audible and speaks with intelligence. Intelligence denotes the presence of "mind" that thinks and wills, creates and permeates everything. This positively all powerful possession is the means endowed to everyone to create, invent, and to bring everything into being.

The mind creates on a nanosecond by nanosecond basis. Every day, all day long, minds create paintings, architecture, structures, electronic inventions, etc. which all fall in to the category of matter. Furthermore, authors of novels create characters that are imbued with made up personalities all by using the mind.

Based on the capability of mind, then, it is very likely that God, created the universe, the macrocosm, and man the microcosm, just by virtue of thinking of such enterprises.

This concept that God is mind and the universe is mental was derived from the book, Kybalion, written by the Three Initiates. The Kybalion is a book on hermetic philosophy of which the concept of mind described herein is first of seven hermetic principles.

The Kybalion stipulates that: God is mind - the universe is mental insinuating that the macrocosm and microcosm are products of a phantasmagoria or an illusion.

This segment of the book, God is substantiality, is the judgment and view of the writer. In no way should this view be considered factual but merely fodder for contemplation. This statement adheres to the comment made earlier in the forward segment of this book "no one knows anything about anything for sure."

THE DEVIL

Accepting everything emanates from the mind of <u>God</u>, it is not likely that anything would come from the mind of God that in any way, shape or form would be fitting to be referred to as the Devil as we are led to believe this thing to be.

There is no reason for the establishment of such an entity. The mere mention of the word Devil brings to mind, immediately, an environment of intense heat and fire. Being that "<u>God</u>" as written about earlier in this work, is a consuming "<u>fire</u>" it is not likely that anything else could exist as fire, as it would be a resemblance of "<u>God</u>."

So, if the conclusion is that the "Devil" does not exist, then what would be put in place to substitute for the function to influence the need to transform the <u>coarse</u> to the <u>fine</u> to achieve closeness to God.

Common belief is that disobedience or a violation to the "laws" of "<u>God</u>" results in an impedance and restrictive force which causes an indefinite and/or continuous extension of the duration in achieving closeness to "<u>God</u>."

The soul is a spark from God, and since it comes from God must have infinite existence. The fact that the human body that houses the soul is <u>born</u>, <u>lives</u> and <u>dies</u> does not mean that the spark from God ceases to exist.

These souls or sparks from God, based on the level of obedience to the laws of God fall into various categories of grace. These levels of grace correspond to rungs on a <u>ladder</u>.

The ladder begins at Gods level and extends away. The severity of disobedience and violation of God's laws determines where on the ladder the soul sets. This method of judgment and punishment for the soul's disobedience to the laws of God is fitting and proper as compared to the "Devil Scenario." It is also effective as it allows for continuous incarnations for a "fix" for the ascension up the ladder to get closer and closer to God.

The benefits of being closer to God on the ladder means you have achieved a certain abundance of knowledge in your incarnation voyages that make you eligible to be a "lieutenant" to God to carry out the original plan which is to provide "Heaven" everyone believes in and be relieved of the trials and tribulations that takes place for those souls further down on the ladder.

What the above reflects is that life in this phantasmagoria, this illusion, in the mind of God is continuous and never ending until this substantial substance decides to terminate the contemplating, the concentrating, and the fixating on what it is all can see as far as the eye will permit.

Now then, there are some who will read this narrative and be totally convinced that the author is delirious from smoking the drapes. However, these same individuals when questioned about the mysteries which herein some insight is provided, will be incapable of expressing any intelligent analysis whatsoever.

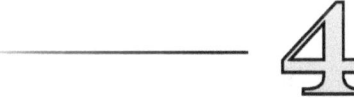

4

THE SMARAGDINE TABLE

Now, I take you away to talk about an essay written by the thrice great Hermes Trismegistis who on a slab of emerald, namely called The Smaragdine Table, engraved an essay which describes the mechanics on which the world was created and the process that was established and put in place for all microcosmic life to follow in order to propagate any and all species and the means to achieve a relationship with the substantiality that was originally intended.

This essay, The Smaragdine Table, contains everything required to understand the plan of the substantiality when put into effect when the universe was contemplated.

Following is my analysis of Hermes magnificent work originally established in Greek translated into Latin and then English.

THE SMARAGDINE TABLE

True, without error, certain and most true; that which is above is as that which is below, and that which is below is as that which is above, for performing the miracles of the One Thing; and as all things are from one, by the mediation of one, so all things arose from this one thing by adaptation; the father of it is the Sun, the mother of it is the moon; the Wind carried it in its belly; the name thereof is the Earth. This is the father of all perfection, on consummation of the whole world. The power of it is integral, if it turned into earth. Thou shalt separate the earth from the fine, the subtle from the gross, gently, with much sagacity, it ascends from earth to heaven, and again descends from heaven to earth; and revives the strength of the superiors and of the inferiors. So thou hast the glory of the whole world; therefore let all obscurity flee before thee. This is the strong fortitude of all fortitudes, overcoming every subtle, and penetrating every solid, thing. So the world was created. Hence were all wonderful adaptations of which this is the manner. Therefore I am called Thrice Great Hermes, having the three parts of the Philosophy of the whole world. That which I have written in consummated concerning the Operation of the Sun.

5

THE SMARAGDINE
TABLE ANALYSIS

"True without error, certain and most true; that which is <u>above</u> is as that which is <u>below</u>, and that which is <u>below</u> is as that which is <u>above</u>." This choice of words instills in the reader that the commentary is valid and cannot be doubted.

Accepting the premise that the commentary is valid, one must then contemplate just to what the <u>above</u> and <u>below</u> relates.

Following are definitions of above and below taken from the Century Dictionary:

<blockquote>

Above – in open site or over

Below – under or beneath

</blockquote>

In trying to arrive at a meaningful understanding of the definition "<u>in open site</u>" or "<u>over</u>" for <u>above</u> it is likely that one could conclude that the <u>universe</u>, the <u>macrocosm</u>, fits the description of being "<u>in open site</u>" or "<u>over</u>" everything.

The definition of <u>below</u>, "<u>under or beneath</u>", suggests <u>the below</u> is <u>under</u> or <u>beneath</u> the above or <u>the universe</u> and shares a common characteristics that is an exact copy of <u>the above</u>.

Considering the universe to be the above and the below to contain an exact copy of the above, then what is in the below that shares a typical characteristic of the above?

In examining the universe, the above, it is apparent that "in open site" there are a multitude of spherical objects whirling around by themselves and each other. True, without error, certain and most true, this characteristic would be agreed upon to be obvious and foremost.

Therefore, in view of this obviety, the manner in which the universe, the above, is structured fashions the model which is typical in the below. This being the case, it is difficult to conceive what in the below is typical of this model especially when viewing the above enormity and magnitude.

However, since the below is within the above it becomes plausible that a copy of the above model could exist in the below in a lesser degree of magnitude.

In search of the below for a copy of the structural model of the above, one finds that the earthly body is an exact duplicate of this geometrical arrangement of spherical objects. The earthly body is comprised of atoms, corpuscles, neutrons, protons, whirling around each other and themselves. This likeness substantiates the claim as above so below and as below so above.

The Smaragdine Table continued: *"for performing miracles of the one thing; and as all things are from one by the mediation of one, so all things arose from this one thing by adaptation;"*

It should be borne in mind, that the structural likeness between the above and below exists everywhere regardless of size and establishes the compatibility and integration of parts from above to below for the propagation of additional earthly bodies (life) through the adaptation of the "one thing" from which all things arise and become through an act of perfection, a medium establishing a miraculous outcome.

The Smaragdine Table continued: *"the father of "it" (the one thing) is the sun, the mother of "it" (the one thing) is the moon; the wind carried "it" in it belly, the name thereof (the one thing) is the earth."*

This passage describes the structure of the "one thing." The passage indicates that the sun or fire is the father of the one thing, the positive pole of the component. The moon or water is the mother of the one thing, the negative pole of the component. This positive and negative pole comprise the composition of the atom or differently named monad which is a spark from God. This atom is carried by the wind from above to below where it is inhaled by an earthly body and through an act of perfection, propagation begins. This entire plot involves all four elements; fire, air, water, earth.

The Smaragdine Talbe continued: *"this is the father (act) of all perfection, on consummation of the whole world. The power of it (the act of perfection) is integral, if it (the act of perfection) turned into earth."*

This act of perfection is a manifestation of power only when and if the integrated parts suited for the subservience of a vital process transforms the "one thing," a spark from God into a living earth body or microcosm.

The marriage of the integrated parts and implementation of the vital process is in the fulfillment of the whole world, meaning that this process relates to all things, anywhere, and everywhere in the universe or macrocosm.

The Smaragdine Table continues: *"Thou shalt separate the earth from the fine, the subtle from the gross, gently, with much sagacity: "it" ascends from earth to heaven, and descends from heaven to earth; and revives the strength of the superiors and of the inferiors."*

Man must separate the mundane (earth) from the pure (fire), the perfect from the sensual, in a refined manner with a great deal of wisdom.

Through the correct use of the sacred gifts of life, which include free will, the consciousness of man in the microcosm (earth) identifies with the consciousness of God the macrocosm.

This identity includes a flow upward from the microcosm with aspirations of lesser perfection to the macrocosm for an exchange of virtues and then flows downward again to the microcosm.

This exchange takes place for the benefit of all levels of life in pursuit to perfection and closeness to God. This is the open door which no man can shut.

The Smaragdine Table continues: *"So thou hast the glory of the whole world; therefore let all obscurity flee before thee. This is the strong fortitude of all fortitudes, overcoming every subtle, and penetrating every solid, thing. So the world was created. Hence were all wonderful adaptations of which this is the manner."*

The teaching of the Smaragdine Table thus far exhibits the glory of the whole world. These teachings unfold as the majesty splendor, and bliss contained in the universe through the mind of God. These teachings are extended to remove all doubt about the intention of any activity that may be sly and underhanded. These teachings are intended also to provide capability and power to comprehend the difference between, and grasping the understanding of every serious and reliable vision of an impractical nature.

The teachings relate to how the world was created and how the free flow of sparks from God is the basic fundamental mechanism for the establishment of everything, everywhere and continues to be wherever and whenever ADAPTABLE.

Furthermore, since all things are from one, by the mediation of one, and all things arose from an adaptation of the one thing then it would be wise to say that: "true without error, certain and most true; that which is above is as that which is below and that which is below is as that which is above."

ADDENDUM TO THE
SMARAGDINE TABLE ANALYSIS

Whenever, God thought, everything became. Everything that became, became having the same integrated structural arrangement of components.

This compatibility is the fundamental foundation that allows more similar becomings to become through the adaptabilities of the coming or sparks from God which are reflections and mirror images of the same integrated structure arrangement of what already has become from God's thoughts.

This spark from God is the one thing that Hermes speaks about in the Smaragdine table.

Since everything that has become through the thoughts of God, is as everything else that has become, becomes whatever is anywhere, and is everything everywhere or as Hermes put it as above so below.

All things from God are constructed in the same manner; i.e. atoms whirling around themselves and each other.

This basic fundamental likeness is the construction blueprint for everything, anywhere, everywhere, and manifests itself in several levels of being or a series of interpenetrating cosmic fields, and designated as planes of correspondence.

These levels of being vary from one another only by the fundamental unit of energy measurement.

The levels of being are:

1. The field of matter – the physical body

2. The field of mind or mental body

3. The casual field – the casual body

After many attempts to produce an analysis of the Smaragdine table, it is my opinion that the analysis offered above is accurate and authentic. Once the reader becomes acquainted with the fact that everything is made up of the same structure then this emphasis becomes placed on the trigger that sets everything in motion that causes repeated activity creating multiples of any particular species.

Since the light we realize on earth stems from the sun which is a ball of fire and shedding sparks on a continuous basis, it is not difficult to speculate that God is a spiritual consuming fire shedding sparks continuously. As all things are composed of the same structure, it is not far-fetched to arrive at the conception that these sparks from God are atoms made up of electrons and protons. There are a multitude of these sparks floating in the atmosphere and get carried to earth and elsewhere to act as the seed of a beginning.

When God was alone, the sparks were essentially inert as nothing existed to trigger any actions. So God thought about man and woman, plus and minus, wharf and woof, and lo and behold the sparks now have a target to penetrate. In thinking about man and woman, they became and although these sparks are inhaled by this man and woman, the trigger to energize the spark was forbidden to them (the apple). Forbidden to them in the sense that as long as they controlled their emotions, everything needed to sustain themselves was available always.

However, the negative pole, the woman became overcome by an emotion of desire and enticed the positive pole, the man, to perform the act of perfection that triggered the spark from God to germinate and then there were three. This lack of control of desire was the beginning of producing more of the man and woman that were the result of God's thoughts. Additional, man and woman were no longer a product of God's thoughts. Man and Woman began propagation through the act of perfection that triggered the one thing, a spark from God.

7

WHAT ARE WE?

One day while contemplating, I came upon the transfiguration of Jesus. I began to think about the event and it dawned on me that Peter, James and John who were with Jesus at that time claimed to have seen Jesus talking to Moses and Elijah. What popped into my head was, how did these guys recognize Moses and Elijah since they never saw them before. Moreover, since Moses and Elijah were not living, how is it that their bodies were intact for these three guys to recognize them?

It was peculiar to read that two people were dead appeared in their bodies. I thought that when people die their bodies are left to decay and become granulated matter or dust. I'm sure that this transformation took place as I suspect it was when Jesus became fully enlightened, soul conscious, an initiate, and all the other words that describe atonement with God.

My mind immediately switched from this event to the ascension of Jesus into the sky. The ascension into the stratosphere suggests that he having been crucified and pronounced dead and resurrected was off to somewhere in his earthly body which again indicated that Jesus' life on earth was ended and returns to somewhere. This rising into the sky certainly suggests again that Jesus was dead, but if you are dead doesn't the body have to be left on the planet earth?

So you see, we are faced with a paradox. Everybody that lives and dies leaves their bodies here on earth meaning that the something that is you continues to exist in some form whatever that may be. Yet Peter, James and John claimed to have seen Moses and Elijah in their earthly bodies.

Now whether or not these guys saw what they saw at the transfiguration, and what was seen at the ascension, does not alter the fact that as we know it today when you die your body remains on earth and the something called you continues to exist. But what is that something?

Now according to the analysis of the Smaragdine table offered in this book, we are sparks from God. Therefore, being a part of God, this something must be infinite. So the fact that this something is a part of God and infinite, this something must be something substantial.

Now, what is it that is something substantial? What exists when the body dies? Hermes Trismegistis teaches that God is mind and the universe in mental, therefore, it is likely and conceivable that the something that remains after death is the "mind" which the dictionary indicates is the synonym for the soul.

So, the spark from God, the mind, and the soul are one. We know from the analysis of the Smaragdine table that everything everywhere is constructed in the same fashion i.e. whirling spheres revolving around and about each other. The spark from God is essentially an atom suggesting that the soul, the mind, is constructed similarly, i.e. a multitude of protons and electrons whirling around each other. This model of construction typifies the technology exhibited in semi-conductors whereby the processing of various materials such as silicon to enhance the electrons inherent in the material allows storage of data which everyone refers to as memory. Knowingly, gigabytes of memory can be stored in minute areas of this material.

Therefore, it can be conceived that the mind, soul or memory body must have infinite storage capacity explaining how it is possible to retain all knowledge from previous incarnations.

Now that we think we have surmised what the soul, mind, memory body can do and what its function is, what does it look like?

Since atoms are invisible to the naked eye and the soul, mind, memory body are composed of atoms then this substantial entity must be invisible. Does it have form? If so, what is it? I really don't know.

I visualize this memory body as being a ball of energy with electrons whirling about in many different orbits tightly spaced so that there is barely room between each and every orbital path.

What I have just explained makes rational sense to me as I can visualize every aspect of the model being possible.

The role of life and death tends to explain how when a multitude of lives are lost during a catastrophic event or a war similar to the wars when masses of man lined up and charged at one another killing thousands or people at any one time. It almost makes you feel that God took this condition into consideration when contemplating this illusion of which we are a part, as the lives lost are merely loss of bodies that will ultimately return to the journey of achieving perfection which was the original intent of God in the first place.

I offer no explanation as to why the loss of family members and loved ones occurs and how the relationship that exists between them becomes discontinued as a result of their demise.

I am having a difficult time believing that when people die off there is an expectation of meeting their loved ones no matter what the relationship, in that somewhere that is never defined. Can you imagine sons, daughters meeting their moms, dads, whenever, wherever, in a chain of families that have gone on for centuries? Could this be possible?

If so, where? To do what? For how long? What would be the motivation to exist?

It is my belief that God always was, whatever that means and always will be, whatever that means. God always was and always will be means to me that whatever God is, and we hear and read that God shows up as a fire, can only be an endless process of something that regenerates constantly in never ending cycles. Isn't that the process created for us through incarnation time after time, until we get the formula for becoming perfect as God is, to be God like in reality which set up a reincarnation cycle with these people of perfection to further advance whatever in this world that improves living to the original garden of eden qualities which I'm not so sure I fully understand the purpose of this eutopia in the first place.

When it comes to the question as to why God contemplated the universe, Hermes Trismegistis had no answer and tightly pressed his lips together preventing him from responding to the question.

Being always and possessing the capability of mentally conjuring up anything at one time, anywhere, it is difficult to conceive why this substantial reality would "dream up" such a scenario that I am writing about in this work. Except for the fact that what is visualized and realized in this phantasmagoria is exceptionally beautiful, perfect in every respect, continuous and never ending, and extends opportunity to excel in anything that can be conceived just by obeying certain laws and separating the coarse from the fine in a manner that coincides with the mind of God. I could not think of a better illusion to contemplate.

LOVE

Love is a word frequently used to express the liking of something. It is bantered around loosely to indicate that someone is pleased with something. This something could be anything, absolutely anything, that falls into any aspect of life and the individual using the word does not on many occasions have the foggiest idea of exactly what he or she is saying but is confident that the expression of love for whatever makes the point that he or she is pleased with the whatever.

In my opinion love is a magical word. Love is a word that cannot be fully explained in a way that will be fully absorbed mentally because "true love' connotes a feeling that cannot be completely described so that it can be felt by others as it is felt by the beholder of the feeling being felt.

If this feeling of love could be realized by all, then all the degrading aspects, yes all aspects, would cease to exist because the rapture of the feeling is so powerfully captivating that the need for any other whatever that tends toward these degrading aspects would be totally unnecessary.

What is this thing called love? Love is the ultimate emotion when felt as designed to be felt and identified as really true love and is a state of bliss that can only be described by the beholder. Love is a feeling that is not the same as the false ecstasy produced from loves opponent, lust, which many would make a wager is the feeling of love. Wrong! Lust is the opposite pole of love.

The stark difference between lust and love is tantamount to the two opposite poles, hot and cold. The contrast between these two models is that the individual can easily determine the difference between hot and cold that is absolute, but because lust and love produce a sensation that is disguised to the beholder makes it difficult to distinguish one from the other at the time this emotion emerges.

When the feeling of love is really realized, the sexual embrace is performed in a manner where the two participants engage in this act with total unselfishness and with thoughts that they, while in the throes of this act are one, making the performance an act of perfection bringing them closer to God.

LIVING LIFE

What is life all about? Life is an opportunity! You say, an opportunity for what? I say an opportunity to get closer to God. You say what will getting closer to God buy me? I say getting closer to God is better than being further away from God, regardless whether we know exactly what is the difference.

Have you considered what awaits you after your demise and your soul leaves your body? Do you think that being closer to God makes you eligible for whatever as compared to being further away from God? I think so! I believe being close to God makes you eligible to reincarnate to make a significant contribution to this phantasmagoria, this illusion that God has mentally established in so perfect a manner for the very purpose of beauty wherever, and forever. Don't you think that people who achieve perfection in life regardless of what they do isn't a privilege granted to them for obeying the rules of God? I believe your reincarnation is representative of your action in previous lives whether the activity was good or bad.

Certainly this is an explanation of heaven that makes sense. All these explanations of heaven being some wonderland that cannot be or understood, to me is not a rational comprehension and not believable.

God in establishing everything everywhere and knows everything about everything except one thing and that is just what you are going to do regarding the free will granted to you upon arrival on this earth. This granting you free will to do as you see fit to carry out life put you in a position to determine your own destiny. Therefore, by just choosing the right fork in the road you set the stage to be eligible and privileged to carry out something for God which I'm sure is to provide absolutely more beauty to this finite ever-becoming phantasmagoria.

God, who conjured up the macrocosm and microcosm better known as the universe and man, mentally confirmed the stages for everything imaginable which should be adequate for the microcosm to use to play out the drama that will ultimately lead to God like qualities that will be used to assist in making this illusional scene what everybody expects heaven to be whenever.

10

THE SOUL

The soul, the soul, the soul! We all hear talk about the soul. Just what is this soul?

My Sunday school teacher portrayed the soul as being white and every time an offense (sin) against the law of God was committed a black spot or mark was placed upon the soul. I for the like of me, could never understand what this was all about. First of all, I could never visualize what this white whatever is. Does the soul look as I physically appear in life? Does it speak, see, eat, walk, what? Totally bewildering, and definitely a conundrum.

After many years of reading everything I could get my hands on regarding subjects related to the soul, I have come to realize the soul as a miniature universe. This miniature universe appears to be an electrical field, not solid in form. This electrical field is violet in color with many spheres orbiting around something not identifiable and almost transparent and would be if this unidentifiable object in the center were not there.

What I have just described is similar to an electrical field of electrons whirling around themselves and the unidentifiable center object.

In studying the aura, the electrical field surrounding everything, it dawned on me that the auric electrical field may just be what I described as being the soul. The center of the aura is indeed whatever the aura surrounds. In the case of a person, that person is the center around which all the spherical objects whirl.

So, is it possible that the aura really is the soul?

Since the macrocosm and microcosm are carbon copies of one another structurally (see the analysis of the Smaragdine table, this book) and since the soul is the invisible representative of the body, why wouldn't the aura being structurally the same as the micro and macrocosm be the soul? Yes? No? Sounds plausible to me until a theory of some other reasoning comes forth to discount this one.

I trust that my version of what the soul may be does not send anyone off into an outburst of denunciation and disbelief because that was not the intent.

However, if whoever becomes affected in this manner has anything to offer regarding the soul, it would be best to publish an essay which may affect others similarly. Furthermore, prior to publishing such an essay, the adage, "what is it you know for sure?" should be pondered.

It is recognized that this short dissertation on the subject of the soul does not truly reflect adequate light to be totally convincing. My anxiety prevailed to share this version with someone.

11

PINOCCHIO

Every once in a while something comes along that matches the drama of life. To me the story of Pinocchio is a perfect example of that mystery.

The story of Pinocchio is about a cobbler, named Gepeto. Gepeto without children decides to construct a marionette, a puppet, to fill that void.

This is similar to God creating Adam. Pinocchio functions as a little boy and is taught that he must always tell the truth, otherwise his nose will grow longer every time he disobeys the rule.

This arrangement appears to be similar to disobeying to the laws of God to prevent the soul from drifting further and further away from God.

In order to assist Pinocchio to use his free will in making decisions, a cricket called Jiminy is assigned to act as Pinocchio's conscious. Jiminy Cricket speaks with Pinocchio on all matters regarding right and wrong and then leaves the decision making up to Pinocchio.

This Jiminy Cricket character is tantamount to the voice we hear continuously whispering to us when faced with deciding right from wrong. As Hermes Trismegisitis put it, "trying to separate the coarse from the fine." (see the Smaragdine table, this book)

Pinocchio on several occasions discounts the advice given to him by Jiminy Cricket and watches his nose grow longer.

Pinocchio finally recognizes that ignoring the advice given to him by his conscious, Jiminy Cricket, is certainly not the path to be on watching his nose grow longer. Pinocchio perceives that accepting the advice of his conscious will absolutely lead to becoming real and no longer a puppet.

This scenario is the model that must be pursued in order to achieve enlightenment. The sooner it is recognized that separating the coarse from the fine on a continuous basis, the sooner the light will come on and provide the understanding of all obscurities we so wantingly want to uncover.

By virtue of the fact that the story of Pinocchio was written smacks of the probability that the writer of the story shares the philosophy expressed in this essay and book.

To this statement must be added: "you never know to whom you are talking."

If anything is gleaned from the story of Pinocchio it must be that God knows everything except what branch of the fork in the road you will take by virtue of the gift to you of free will.

12

NATURE, BODY, SPIRIT, SOUL, ENLIGHTENMENT, THE FOUR NOBLE TRUTHS, THE UNIVERSE

Nature is: the birthplace of all affection, the tomb of all evil, the primary school of human souls, the purification of the virtues, the gymnasia of thought, a plane inclined beginning at instinct and ending in omniscience, the telegraphic system of all being connecting its remotest point, the work shop of the infinite and eternal God, the grand orchestra of all symphonies, the ladder reaching from nonentity to the dome beneath which sits the law maker of the universe.

Body is purely material, tangible, dense, weighable, atomical or particled.

Spirit is made up of three parts: 1) It interpenetrates, flows through and form, and makes up the life of material existence. 2) It is the medium in which the universe floats and has its being but vastly different from 1 3) It is mental productivity and the results there from such as thoughts.

Soul is a stately principle that thinks, feels, tastes, sees, knows, aspires, suffers, hates, loves, fears, calculates and enjoys.

Soul is a thing, sui generis (self-character), and unique. Sight, taste, and the senses are some of the souls properties. Reflection, reason and imagination are some soul qualities. Judgment is a soul prerogative. Physical senses the soul's drama. Earthly experience is the school of the soul. The second life is the university from whense the soul graduates.

Enlightenment is a state of purity on the spiritual, mental and physical planes. Purity raises the physical vibrational frequency that is above and distinguishable from the masses and furnishes an awakened understanding of the obscurities that are expounded upon in this work. Purity is attained by correct breathing practices, foods consumed, body cleanliness, mind cleanliness and moral conviction and practices and adherence to the ten commandments.

Enlightenment awaits everyone. The enlightenment path begins when it becomes evident that there is more than what is currently believed and therefore a search begins to discover what it takes to achieve that end.

In studying the Buddha, a lesson that may clearly reveal the evidence needed to follow the path to a higher self. Following is the passage, "The Four Noble Truths."

What is the noble truth of suffering? Birth is suffering, decay is suffering, death is suffering, sorrow, lamentation, pain, grief and despair are suffering, not to get what one desires is suffering, in short the 5 groups of existence are suffering.

What now is the noble truth of the origin of suffering? It is the craving which gives rise to fresh rebirth and bound up with pleasure and lust, none here, none there, finds every fresh delight. But where does this craving arise and take root? Wherever in the world there are delightful and pleasurable things, there this craving rises and takes root. Eye, ear, tongue, body, and mind are delightful and pleasurable; there this craving arises and takes root.

Visual objects, sounds, smells, tastes, bodily impressions, and mind objects are delightful and pleasurable; there this craving arises and takes root.

Consciousness, sense impressions, feeling born of sense impressions, perception, will, craving, thinking and reflection are delightful and pleasurable; there this craving arises and takes root.

What now is the noble truth of the extinction of suffering? It is the complete fading away and extinction of this craving, its forsaking and abandonment, liberation and detachment from it. The extinction of greed, hate, delusion; this indeed is called nirvana.

And for a disciple thus freed, in whose heart dwells peace, there is nothing to be added to what has been, and naught more remains to do. Just as a rock of one solid mass remains unshaken by the wind, even so neither forms, nor sounds, nor odors, nor tastes, nor contacts of any kind, neither the desired, nor the undesired can cause such a one to waver, one is steadfast in mind, gained in deliverance.

And one who has considered all the contrasts of this earth, and is no more disturbed by anything whatever in the world, the peaceful one, freed from rage, from sorrow, and from longing, has passed beyond birth and decay.

This I call neither arising, nor passing away, neither standing still, nor being born, nor dying. There is neither foothold, nor development, nor any basis. This is the end of suffering.

Hence, the purpose of the holy life does not consist in acquiring alms, honor, or fame, nor in gaining morality, concentration, or the eye of knowledge. That unshakable deliverance of the heart: that indeed is the object of the holy life, that is the essence, that is its goal.

What now is the noble truth of the path that leads to the extinction of suffering?

To give oneself up to indulgence in sensual pleasure, the base, common, vulgar, unholy, unprofitable, or to give oneself up to self-mortification, the painful, unholy, unprofitable, both these two extremes, the perfect one has avoided and has found out the middle path, which makes one both see and know, which leads to peace, to discernment, to nirvana. It is the noble eight fold path that leads to the extinction of suffering, namely:

1) right understanding
2) right thought
3) right speech
4) right action

5) right livelihood
6) right effort
7) right mindfulness
8) right concentration

This is the middle path which the perfect one has found out, which makes one both see and know, which leads to discernment, to enlightenment.

The universe is the result of God's meditative thoughts. The universe, its laws, its powers, its life, its phenomina are all realized from a state of mediation and/or dream, illusion, a phantasmagoria.

To all that is finite, the universe must be treated as real. Life action, and thought must be based on the universe being real, with an understanding that the truth of the universe is a dream with life actions and thought having its own laws and levels.

Anything having a beginning and an end must be unreal and untrue. Therefore, from the absolute point of view, nothing is real except God.

Enlightenment is a state of mind, that corresponds to the mind of God on all planes of existence, i.e. the physical, the mental, the spiritual , the emotional or soulular.

The creative process is called involution, the involuntary stage of creation or the out-drawing of divine energy. The evolution state of creation is called the in-drawing, the going back to God, or the return swing of the pendulum.

13

RANDOM GLOSSARY OF WORDS

Obscurities – something unknown but may be brought to light.

Mysterious – contains something unknown.

Abstruse – difficult to understand because of its complexity or profundity.

Esoteric – understood by a small group possessing special knowledge.

Mysticism – belief that through contemplating and love, man can achieve a direct and immediate consciousness of God or of divine truth.

Compilation – a gathering of literary materials in a book.

Intuition – perception without reason.

Contemplate – to mediate.

Concentrate – bring to bear on one point or object.

Fixate – to be unchangeable in purpose or conviction.

The Winged Globe – a house of many mansion.

To be taught is to believe – to experience is know absolutely

Mitigate – punishment.

Prescient – fore-knowledge.

Consciousness – the voice of God in the soul.

Imagination – the creative faculty of man, man's invisible work shop, comes from the heart.

Astronomy – denotes wisdom.

The Inner Sight – awakening of the subconscious.

Harmony – a well-balanced, union of body, mind and spirit.

Self-Control – the measure of Godhood.

Sternity – today.

A Death Trance– the sleep of Sialam (Marie Corelli)

Animus – mind, feeling, will.

Anima – air, breath, soul, mind.

God is positive heat. The aura of Diety is love

- The primary element of power

- The external fire sphere

- The pulse of matter

- The introduction of love is crystalline

Only time is necessary to refine love into spiritual essence.

The soul is feminine – the divine Sophia.

Inscrutable – impenetrable, unfathomable, incomprehensible, mysterious.

ABOUT THE AUTHOR

Trebor Onairtas was born of immigrants during the Great Depression. He was educated in the field of engineering and participated in the development of the Distant Early Warning Radar System, the first satellite to generate its own electrical power source, as well as the Talos Missile System. He holds many US patents related to power semiconductor products.

Married and father of two children, he lives in Allmauchy, New Jersey. He became interested in the arcane philosophies in the mid-1950s and has been studying various related philosophies ever since with extra special attention devoted to the Hermetic philosophy.

The desire to share the accumulated knowledge gleaned from years of study on this subject lead to the publication of this book.

www.ingramcontent.com/pod-product-compliance
Lightning Source LLC
Chambersburg PA
CBHW050343290526
45785CB00006B/2619